After Another Chance Inspirational Poems, Quotes & Testimonies

Volume 2

By

Dorothy A. Cooper

After Another Chance

Inspirational Poems, Quotes & Testimonies

Volume 2

Copyright © February 2014

Dorothy A. Cooper

Dorothy A. Cooper is published under the umbrella

Of

Katrinasworks.com

DEDICATION

Your determination for me to know the TRUTH is the reason for my transformed mind, my renewed spirit, my dedicated soul. At a time when my way was dark and dreary, it was you who kept coming to my rescue. You were the one who kept tugging on me and telling me to get up and don't give up! When there was no strength left in my body to get up and get dressed to face the day, by my hand, you would take me and guide me, reassuring me the entire way, everything would be okay, if I just keep the faith.

There were so many nights of crying and praying. Even though I felt all alone, never was I really because I could feel your spirit in the room with me. Bringing comfort, yes you did. Ministering unto my soul. Not letting me feel sorry for my situation. I could literally feel you holding me. It was the peace needed in order to finally close my tired eyes and rest so I would be prepared enough to face the agony all over again the very next day.

God, through Jesus, thank You! Thank You for the trial! Thank You for the purging of my soul! Hallelujah! Thank You for the dark times, for it taught me how to see! Thank You, Father for the lonely times, for they taught me how to love unconditionally! Thank You for the times I prayed and right away You did not answer, for it taught me not only patience, Father, but unyielding obedience to Your will and Your way! Thank You Father, God for choosing me to mold, to deliver, to save, just so You could have a relationship with me!

With all of my renewed heart and made up mind, God, through Christ Jesus, I humbly dedicate "After Another Chance", Inspirational Poems, Songs, Quotes & Testimonies, Volume 2, to the both of You. You are the reason for "Another Chance", and "After Another Chance", has been granted, understanding comes to the fact, none of it would be possible without You God, through, Christ Jesus. Without further ado, I present, "After Another Chance"....

~Amen~

A HEART TO HEART WITH GOD

Lord, what is it that You would have me to say
To Your people, that has not already been said
By so many others before me? Lord, what is it,
Father, that You sir, would have me to say to
My brothers and sisters that would bring
Understanding to Who and What You really are?
Why is it so hard to see it is certainly not this pagan
God in which so many knees seems to keep falling
Down and praying to for money, fancy cars, big houses?
Father, can You please remove the stick from mine
Eyes? Evidently one is still there because it is difficult
To understand why professed believers in You,
Really do not understand power at all.

Father, they do not want to hear the truth. Your
Children are perishing for lack of knowledge!
Your children would rather hear a lie; then the
Truth. Do not You see their reactions when
Proclaiming what thus saith the Lord to them?
I ask only these questions, Father God, because
My faith is already so grounded in You. Rooted
In Your awesome power is my sincere desire to do
Things Your way! I shall not be tossed and blown!
I have made my mind up to not just serve You, Lord,
But, serve with a pure heart, one full of gladness!

However; why then, oh Gracious One, does it seem
The ones being rewarded are the very ones openly
Being defiant to Your very dialect! Your laws,
Statues and let us not forget commandments; which
By the way the whole duty of man is to fear You and
Keep Your commandments? I'm having a heart to
Heart with You Master! That's all! Same thing so many
Before me have done and I do not know how many more
Servants after me, will do, for the earthquakes in diver's
Places are becoming more frequent. Hearing of actual wars,
As well as rumors of wars, are taking place; just like You

Stated in 1 Timothy; signifying, may I add the
Coming back of Your only begotten son, Christ Jesus!
Which by the way, You're not sending Him back to throw
A party!

So, again I ask Master, if your people did not listen in
The past, if all of the signs and wonders in which You have
Already allowed to happen such as tornadoes and floods
Wiping out big mega towns in a matter of minutes, then
What Father, what am I to say? Who am I to say it?
Because whenever I do say it Father; ignorance is shown
Through the jokes being made as to how You said for
Me to say it! Hatred, discord, expressions of being disgruntled
Begins to happen just like it did at the cross, Father,
Many, many, centuries ago!

Why must I be the one who has to die or be killed by the
Hands of Your disobedient children when I am doing all
I can to strive daily to serve You? Is not all of my
Sacrificing which is being made honored in Your eyesight
Sir, as a good and faithful servant? Jesus can You help me
Understand please? Can You ask our Father these things
For me? Please? I know You know I mean no harm at
All by asking these questions. I know You know my
Heart. The place in which You judge daily the debt of
My love for You both. Forgive me if I am wrong, Lord,
For I too once used to be ignorant, until You, Oh Holy One,
Lead me straight into the studying of Your most Holy Words?

So I guess I will continue to allow you to use me for Your story,
Master, and never for my glory! Thank You, Almighty,
For the Heart to Heart! I'm feeling better already!

~Amen~

ABIDE IN ME SWEET JESUS

Abide in me, sweet Jesus.
With Your favor, fill me up

Abide in me, oh Precious One.
So, of Your glory, I can't get enough!
Cradle me in Your arms;
As You surround me with the warmth of Your blood.
Oh! Oh! Abide in me, sweet Jesus;
As You fill my heart, with Your love!

ADDICTED

By bringing calm to my fears
Almost a stalker I am
Because of the way I overwhelm
Your existence with my belief in You
For I cannot make it through I am addicted to Your power
I cannot get enough of Your love
To feel the warmth of Your presence
Makes me feel so beautiful!
I am so wrapped up in the thought of You
I get so lost when thinking of You too
One touch from You enlightens my faith
By providing proof there must be God
For only God can bring such joy to my heart!
I am addicted to the way You care
To the way You are always there
Answering my prayers

This thing called life without You
I tried and it was too hard to do
Oh yes, it's true
I am addicted to You Jesus
Everything about You makes my heart sing
A song of praise
A repeating melody of thanks
For Your Amazing ways and grace
It is definitely real this feeling I feel
For continuously all the things You do
Is more than enough proof
You are addicted to me too!

AFTER ANOTHER CHANCE

Believer, before another chance
Can be granted to you by God
To be an obedient and willing servant
Walking by His laws
All iniquity must be removed from the heart
So unselfishly serving others
Become your main thoughts.
Also must be removed
All things in the spirit not like His Son
Because there can be nothing to stop
His work from getting done.
All sin must be seen striving to come to an end
Leaving no desire to disobey His will again.

Believer, to be granted another chance by God
Is a very serious act one very difficult to perform
For the heart must undergo a reconstruction
To get rid of all unsightly self-destruction.
Then a passing must take place of a very difficult test
To remove lessons learned while wandering in the wilderness.
Once conquered, however, the soul is no better
Than others once stood among.
The only difference, believer
Is old ways have been dipped, cleansed, and transformed.

Because After Another Chance, receiver
Has been granted to you by God
The choice has already been made to obey His voice
By no longer being distracted, by no longer being impacted
By any nonspiritual noise.
For the path is now righteous
From which the feet walks upon.
And a new creature, yes
Is what the Beholder now sees.
One ready to diligently and faithfully fight
To fulfill its spiritual duties.
Which means understanding knows

Everything done is never about own selfish needs
But making sure, with your labor, God through Jesus is well pleased.

Therefore, hold on believer
In its power, keep the faith, no matter what, achiever
Because being acceptable to God's plan
Means the new heart understands
It is a blessing to be chosen
To walk in the favor received from God's hands
But only After Another Chance.

ALL OF ME

I gave you my heart Lord
So You could change its beat
I gave You my mind Lord
So You could change how it thinks
From the crown of my head
All the way down to the sole of my feet
I place in Your hands
Lord so You can change
All of me

All of me
All of me
I place in Your hands
Lord so You can change
All of me

I gave You my eyes Lord
So You could change how I see
I gave You my soul Master
Now in Your power it believes
From the crown of my head
All the way down to the sole of my feet
I place in Your hands
Lord so You can change
All of me

All of me
All of me
I place in Your hands
Lord so You can change
All of me

ALL THINGS NOT LIKE YOU ARE GONE

Lord encamp Your spirit
All in this space
Your Holy Spirit
All in this place
Until all things
Not like You are gone

Fill it with Your mercy
Fill it with Your grace
Fill it with Your power
All in this place
Until all things
Not like You, are gone

Lord we need Your favor
All in this place
Lord we need Your healing
All in this place
Until all things
Not like You are gone

Every tear
Every pain
Every desire
Yes Lord everything
Until all things
Not like You are gone

BEFORE THE KING WHEN WE GO STAND

It will be about our fellowship
It will be about our relationship
When we go
Stand before the King
It will be about how much we cared
It will be about how much we shared
When we go
Stand before the King!
Before the King! Before the King!
When we go stand before the King!
It won't be about the type car we drive
But it will be about how we lived our lives
When we go
Stand before the King!
Before the King! Before the King!
When we go stand before the King!

DONE FOR MY GOOD

You broke me down
In the middle of transgressions
Could not make a sound
While learning my lesson
It was so painful
All of the agony endured
But now that it is over
I know it was all done for my good
Done for my good is why I went through
Being purged by the Man with the master plan
He saw me struggling in the wilderness
So He reached down and made me confess
And now that it is over
I know it was all done for my good.

EXCEPT DAY 14

One day out of the middle of many,
Love did not just come,
But came with a smile baring gifts;
Suppose it love; that is, for
Many days before this, and possibly thereafter,
Love did not call, love did not text;
Love did not make an effort to come by,
Unless love was in the mood for some loving.
During this missing in action time,
The heart, from which true love flows,
Hurts, greatly from the emptiness,
Of longing to be loved by love.
From longing to be held gently by love.
From wondering is this the way true love supposed to be?
However, true love does not tell time.
True love does not fly in inside of a balloon,
Only to lose its air minutes, hours, or even days later.
True love sticks around every day; not just one.
True love separates, leaving home in the morning;
Then, maneuvers off strong thoughts throughout the day,
Of when it will be time to come back together again!
No matter what number the day is; true love, it's there,
Protecting, providing, enhancing, romancing, giving;
Fulfilling, laughing, crying, believing, hoping and praying,
Because true love is just that, true love!
For, true love does not need a number;
To come along and tell it to activate!
True love stays on ready, at all times;
To do everything in its power to make the love;
Be just as true, yet; effecting, and profound, on today;
As it made the heart of another; to feel, on yesterday!
True love, in other words, is accurate every day;
Except day 14.....

"When the path ahead seems too rough to bare, still keep going, for the way, by the feet of Jesus, has already been prepared."

Dorothy A. Cooper

FATHER PLEASE DON'T EVER LEAVE ME THAT WAY AGAIN

Even though every teardrop molded me
Into the faithful servant I am today
Even though every dark cloud
Taught me how to pray
Father please don't ever leave me
That way again

It was such a lonely time in my life
Couldn't find no peace for my weary mind
Seems to me the more I tried
Things just would not turn out right
Father please don't ever leave me
That way again

Father please don't ever leave me
That way again
Even though I understand
It was done to purge me from my sins
Begging You with everything I am
Father please don't ever leave me
That way again

Thank You for pleading my case Jesus
Thank You for giving me another chance to get it right
Because after another chance is granted
Comes the strength to put up a good fight
Even though I understand
It was done to separate me from my sins
Father please don't ever leave me
That way again

FIGHT ON

When you find yourself
In the middle of a storm
And all around you
Is danger and harm
No matter what you do
Keep the courage
God is there with you
Giving you strength somehow
To fight on through

You've got to fight on
Yes you've got to fight on
Cause your blessings
Are waiting for you
At the end of the storm

Don't give up
Don't give in
Don't let fear win
Because your blessings
Are waiting for you
At the end of the storm

You've got to fight on
Yes you've got to fight on
Cause your blessings
Are waiting for you
At the end of the storm

Find the strength to
Fight on
You can make it through
Fight on
Cause your blessings
Are waiting
At the end of the storm

FIND TIME TO PLAY
WHILE SERVING THE LORD

We must find time to play
In a Godly way
To keep the mind sane
When serving the Lord.
It's not hard to be consumed
When helping others make it through
So find time to play while serving the Lord!

Serving the Lord
Serving the Lord
Find time to play
While serving the Lord
Just make sure what you choose
Of its outcome God approves
As you find time to play
While serving the Lord!

Keep a smile on your face
And a song in your heart
Let peace be your guide
While representing God's love
Whenever the problems of others
Become too much to cover
Take a break and play
While serving the Lord!

Serving the Lord
Serving the Lord
Find time to play
While serving the Lord
Just make sure whatever you do
Jesus is there frolicking too
As you find time to play
While serving the Lord!

FOR ME

Jesus went through it all for me
He took being lied on for me
He endured being crucified for me
Jesus was born into this world for me
Jesus lived His life on earth for me
Then He died for me

I owe Jesus
For every unselfish deed He did
From how He mastered being beaten
To how He humbly bled
Yes, but how do I repay the price?
Is there anything to be done, really
Which can add up to the shame,
The blame, the pain suffered for me?
Before my life is over,
My service to others will help Jesus discover
Just how much appreciation there is
To Him for everything He purposefully went through
Not just for me, but for You too!

owe Jesus
For how He went through it all for me
For all the shame He went through for me

GOD IS TELLING US SOMETHING

God is telling us something!
God is telling us something!
God is telling us something!
God is telling us something!

Are we listening?

Day five, still without lights
But, being awaken by faith let's
Weariness know, everything is alright!
God is trying to tell us something, however,
So, should not we be placing our confidence in Him,
For; keeping it there helps to know;
He is going to come save those of us,
Who diligently seek Him, from out of,
The pits of this blacker than black darkness?
Uplift a song of praise in your heart! Keep it there!
Sing so loud it makes negative thoughts flee;
Then rushes in positive ones, filled with glee.

Meanwhile, have you checked on your neighbor?
Your father? Your mother? What about,
Your sister? Or, what even about your brother?
This too includes any soul considered to be; your enemy!
Have we all made a point to come together?
And pray together? Then show love to the other?
Don't you think we better? Besides, wouldn't this be,
The perfect time, to remove all jealousy, strife, hatred
Of any kind; from the mind, by replacing it, with that
Godly love for each other, that's very hard to find?

After all, why must day six come and see us
In the same predicament as all the others?
Should not we come to discover, not only
Is our Father, who sits high and looks low,
Mighty enough to shut down the blessings;
In which, He bestowed upon a whole city, but,

Yes, also; the Creator, the Builder, the Master of all;
God, is telling us something?

God is telling us something!
God is telling us something!
God is telling us something!
God is telling us something!

Are we listening?

HOW JESUS DIED

When I think about
All of the tears
These eyes have shed
Down through the years
Quickly my sadness subsides
When my mind
Reflects on
How Jesus died!
Holes have never
Been driven in my feet and hands
And a crown of thorns have never
Been forced upon my head
Why then should I complain
When I think about the pain
How Jesus died?
After given another chance
To understand
Now when I cry
It is from the sorrow in my mind of
How Jesus died!

I Am A Bridge

I am a bridge leading to tomorrow.
I have been build to elevate,
Up from yesterday's sorrows!
Connecting from my shaky past.
To a positive future; one build to last.
I am a bridge, yes I am a bridge;
Made by God's hands.

I am a bridge made by God's hands!
Next to the clouds have I been build to stand!
Every bolt, every nail, every screw, every rail,
With a frame built with durability;
So after the strongest storm, still standing I will be.
I am a bridge; yes, I am a bridge,
Made by God's hands!

Under the instructions of His perfect plan -
In front of the skyline is how I expand
So when, the world pays attention to me;
It's the Creator who gets all of the praise!
I am a bridge, yes-I am a bridge;
Made by God's hands!.

I am a bridge made by God's hands!
Next to the clouds have I been build to stand!
Every bolt, every nail, every screw, every rail,
With a frame built with durability;
So after the strongest storm, still standing I will be.
I am a bridge; yes, I am a bridge,
Made by God's hands!

IF WE WOULD JUST BELIEVE

Jesus will give us
Joy for our sorrows
Hope for tomorrow
Double for our troubles

Jesus will give us
Peace to our weary minds
Strength to our weak spines
Favor during trying times

If we would just believe
If we would just believe
With the faith of a mustard seed
Believe in His power

Jesus will give us
More than enough
Of His mercy, of His grace,
Of His Love

If we would just believe
If we would just believe
With the faith of a mustard seed
Believe in His power

IN THE MIDDLE OF MY FAITH

Have you ever wanted to give up
Cause the world's weight got too tough
And of transgressions enough was enough
But out of all the fears that were feared
And out of all the tears that were teared
You stood tall during it all
In the middle of your faith

Cause in the middle of your faith
You knew God was waiting there
To see if you believed in your heart
How much for you, child, He cares
Now because you kept holding on
By praising and worshiping His Son
Today you are standing in your blessings
In the middle of your faith

I sure have had days the body
Was so tired with a soul just as weak
It lead to nights, the mind wanted
To think and not sleep
Until to myself I would say
Even if it's more tribulations
Tomorrow I will be okay
Cause I will be standing
Tall through it all
In the middle of my faith.

Cause in the middle of my faith God is waiting there
Cause I believe in my heart for me He cares
And now because I kept holding on
Even though at times I felt so all alone; all alone
I'm standing in my blessings today
In the middle of my faith.

Yes, in the middle of things hoped for and yet to come

Cause when the road got rough
I never gave up on the Lord
Now I'm standing here today
Deep inside my blessings
Right smack dab in the middle of my faith

In The Reach Of Your Arms

I have come to learn;
When looking for salvation,
It can be found in
The reach of your arms. In fact,
The further your extension gets
Greater are the chances; yeah
Of touching the hem,
Of the Lord's garment!

Peace is in the reach;
Joy is in the reach;
Whatever you seek from Jesus;
Is in the reach of your arms.
Healing is in the reach
Love is in the reach
Whatever you need from Jesus;
Is in the reach of your arms

Deliverance is in the reach!
Rest is in the reach!
Forgiveness is in the reach!
Yes, in the reach of your arms!
Believer, I don't know about you, but;
I'm reaching! I'm reaching! I'm reaching! I'm reaching!
Yes, I'm reaching! I'm reaching! I'm reaching! I'm reaching!
Cause whatever I need from Jesus,
Whatever I seek from Jesus,
Is in the reach; in the reach of my arms.

Oh, I have come to learn;
When looking for salvation,
It's in the reach of your arms!

JESUS THANK YOU FOR CHANGING MY LIFE

Jesus, thank You for changing my life
Thank You for touching my faults and making them right.
You gave me another chance to follow the Light
Thank You Jesus for changing my life!
When you removed my iniquities
It brought a positive change in me
Now even my thoughts think differently
Thank You Jesus for changing my life!
Now all I want to do is serve You
With all of my mind, body and soul
Your goodness, grace and power
I so long to behold!
Thank You Jesus for changing my life!

KNEEL DOWN BEFORE THE KING

Come Kneel down
Kneel down before the King
And give Him all
Give Him all of your praise
Call His name
Call on the mighty name of God
As you kneel down
And give Him all of your praise!
Thank His Son
Thank You Jesus for saving me
As you kneel down
Kneel down before the King!

LORD YOU SAVED ME

Lord, when others counted me out
You were the one who erased
All of my doubts
By fulfilling all of my needs
And shining Your Light
in the darkness
So I could see
You saved me

Oh how the pain hurt
Something terrible
Even more cause there was
No one I could talk to
That is until You came along
And filled my emptiness
With Your love
Now the only reason I exist to be
Is because You saved me

So each day I wake
Up giving You praise
For how back in me
You blew life so I
Could breath
I'm so grateful to You
For how my life
Has made a spiritual change
And it is all because
You saved me
Yes You did, Lord
I love You with all of my heart
Because You saved me

Don't want to imagine
Today where I would be
If You had not thought
It was time to come save me

I'm so grateful to You
For how my life
Has made a spiritual change
And it is all because
You saved me
Yes You did, Lord
I love You with all of my heart
Because, You saved me!

MY MAN

Day in, day out
This frame has laid upon the couch
Waiting patiently to be rescued
By the very list comprised
From the thoughts in my mind
Of you. It's been a long time
But still waited have I
Because of believing your presence
Was near. Somewhere out there.
How will I know you? Easy.
Because your likes will be
The same as mine; even your
Dislikes will be of a similar kind.

There must be strength in the framework.
Every line, curve, precept upon precept; built,
From being made with a substance of durability,
As providing security is secured in its purpose.
After being tested down through the years,
From the storms, being in existence brings;
Today, still standing upright is the position.
In fact, more straight is the form;
Representing both profoundness and endurance.
To the eyes, however, every time the smooth,
But tough exterior is marveled upon,
Immediately, utterance is brought to the mind
Of, how beautiful! How strong! How great!

To capture the attention, first and foremost;
The appearance must prove to be; when seen,
Both intellectual; but yet, with a humble disposition.
The mere reflection of who my desires
Desire to be, for why not? Isn't the only way
Iron can sharpen iron is if both pieces are
Capable of handling the sharpening?
Ask Beyonce Knowles, Angelina Jolie, and yes,

Especially, Michelle Obama, for these ladies know,
The very frame spoken of is not that of an actual building;
But, indeed, and very much so the make-up of "My Man"....

MY SENSES BELONGS TO YOU

I'm going to use this mind You gave me Lord
To concentrate on You!
On all the dreams that You gave me Lord
And how to make them come true.
I'm going to use these hands
You blessed me with to edify my soul!
And I'm going to lift them up;
Every chance I get,
To worship You more and more!
All of my senses Lord belongs to You!
And I'm going to use every last one of them,
To make sure that You know;
I love You!
With all of my heart!
These feet Lord You blessed me with,
Will be used to walk the path carved by You!
This tongue Lord will be used,
To speak of Your Truth.
While these fingers count the blessings,
Left for me as proof;
To what happens when I keep my eyes,
And ears Lord, stayed on You too!
All of my senses Lord belongs to You!
And I'm going to use every last one of them Lord,
To make sure that You know;
I love You
With all of my heart!

"Let the peacefulness of God's power
be your ray of hope during dark times."

Dorothy A. Cooper

NO HEAT, STILL GOT POWER

Going on day four for these old tired eyes,
To be pried open at 4 am in the morn, by the hands;
Of cold's crispiness. Focusing in on my circumference,
Brings a self-examination, to still being alive, meaning;
Everything is already okay. Tears form, however,
From looking over to see my last offspring is sound;
Asleep, signifying no worries and evidently no fears, too.
Proof, also, the leadership example instilled in my soul,
Down through the years, by You God, of do not panic;
In times of adversity, is positively, being passed on,
To not just my children, but; my children's children.

Such a revelation, for immediately, in the darkness,
Silent praising forms upon the lips, a sincere worship;
Of, Lord, I thank You, Master for keeping mine safe!
For keeping my mind straight! To take a breath;
And then, be able to breathe with a sigh of relief, that;
Patience has been learned! Such an understatement!
My Lord! Any doubt which finds itself hanging around,
Trying to add its gloominess to the dreariness in which;
Surrounds this place, can't help but to dissipate, however,
Therefore, melting away like ice, for praise now consumes;
This submissive heart, making the blood run warm,
Bringing total understanding to the fact, any circumstance;
Where there is "no heat, still got power", hallelujah, once the,
Temperature of the Holy Spirit is invited in!

THE LORD SENT ME ON A JOURNEY

The Lord, sent me on a journey
So I would believe in everything He put me through
And so for myself, I could see
Just how good He has been to me.

Oh and on this journey, He guided my footsteps
And He carried me when I was weak.
And He was my mouthpiece when I could not speak.
And He fed me food when I could not eat.

Late in the midnight hour, He sat on my bed
And rubbed my head, even ministered to mind
Told me everything was going to be fine
With time and as long as I keep following His lead.

It was still hard to believe; all of the wisdom received
The scenery from lessons learned was nothing like I perceived
Even stronger in the Lord, however, do I believe
For no one can save my soul like He did
Make it whole like He did, transform it to think
Walk, talk, act like He does and that is by being
Lead by the Holy Spirit of Love.

The Lord sent me on a Journey
And I am so glad He did. For it changed all thoughts
In my head to giving Him praise for the blood
He bled. Thank You Father! Over and over again!
For keeping me sane, for setting me free
The day You Lord sent me on a journey!

PASS IT ON

The same love that God
Keeps extending unto you
Pass it on!
Pass it on!

The same grace, mercy,
And favor too,
Pass it on!
Pass it on!
Pass it on!
Pass it on!

Cause when you pass it on
God smiles down on you!
And your made up mind to serve,
Continuously becomes renewed!

So, pass it on!
Pass it on!

SERVANT

Servant, let God's will be done,
And with the understanding;
It is not the will of your own,
But truly the Lord's alone.
With fear and trembling, serve.
With a made up heart to freely give, serve.
With a made up mind to serve, serve.
With resounding joy, serve.

Let thy feet submissively go,
Without hesitation whenever told, to do;
Even though the path seems scary,
Which instructed to walk through.
Servant listen for the voice of the Lord;
Distinguishing it from the other.
When the Spirit brings revelation it's not Him
Flee from sin immediately, do not go any further.

Always remember servant, you are a representative, now,
Of the Most High King! Which means;
Your countenance should be seen, filled,
With devotedness, with honor, with dignity;
With grace, with love, and humility!
Stay in character at all times, servant,
No matter which may come your way;
Test everything, and about all things, pray!
Making sure not to serve by sight, but by faith!

After all servant, you were chosen,
Long before coming into the Light;
That your heart would not just submissively serve,
But willingly serve with all of your might!
Now go, servant, and as you lead others to salvation,
Let there be no hesitation; just tremendous exaltation
Mixed with much exhilaration, at the mere thought of
Being chosen as a faithful Servant of the Most High King!

SPEAK IT

Never tell yourself
What your mind cannot do
Cause it can do anything
If you just believe
Never tell your eyes
What they cannot see
Cause all things are possible
If you just believe

As long as there is a heartbeat
And a need to live freely
All your dreams can be reality
If you just believe.
So speak it

Never tell your feet
Where they cannot go
Speak it and it shall be so
If you just believe
Never tell your hands
What they cannot do
Cause a boat they build by God's plans
If you just believe

As long as you have faith
Even the size of mustard seed
You can accomplish anything
If you just believe

So go ahead speak it and it shall be done
Speak it and it shall be won
Speak it and you shall overcome
If you just believe

THE ONLY ONE I NEED

Wash me in Your precious blood, Lord!
Fill my heart up with Your love, Lord!
Show me that You are the only One I need.

Be my Light Lord, when it's dark.
Yes, protect me from all hurt and harm.
By shielding me, in Your arms.
O Lord show me that You are
The Only One I need....

Cause, Lord, You are the only One
To show You believe in me
Yes, You are the only One
Who has never left me
To call on Your name alone
Gives me so much peace!
Thank You Lord for showing me
You are the only One I need!

THERE IS ALWAYS A PRAISE IN MY SPIRIT

Way before the storm begins to rise,
Way before there is trouble in my life;
Way before I find myself going through,
There is always a praise in my spirit.

From the very second my eyes open from sleeping,
Regardless to how it is I am feeling.
No matter what to this body the enemy try to do;
There is always a praise in my spirit!

Through the years Lord, You have taught me,
How to keep my eyes stayed on You at all times;
This way when burdens arise, fears get pushed to the side!
Cause there is always a praise in my spirit.

So Lord, I lift up my future right now, unto You!
So all worries, doubts, and tears can be removed;
And replaced Lord, with Your amazing grace,
Cause there is always a praise in my spirit!

Second after second, minute after minute,
Hour after hour, day after day;
No matter what comes my way, I'm ready to face;
Cause there is always a praise;
A powerful and sincere praise,
Oh yes, there is always a praise in my spirit.

TURN TURN IT OVER TO JESUS

When you turn it over to Jesus
Let there be no more worrying
Let there be no more struggling
Let there be no more suffering
Cause when you turn it over to Jesus
There should be no more doubts
That Jesus will work it out!
Let go of all your pain
Place it in the Lord's hands
Don't falter by the way side
By faith keep your stand
Cause when you turn it over to Jesus
There should be no more doubts
Jesus will work it out!
Turn, turn it over to Jesus!

UNTO OUR KING

When the last time comes
To hear the birds chirping
And the warmth of the sunshine
My heart doesn't feel anymore
Please don't cry for me
Cause I will be in glory
Listening to Angels sing
Unto our King

Unto our King
I shall be giving praise
As the angels sing
I shall be calling on His name
So please don't worry about me
Cause I will be okay
Listening to the Angels sing
Unto our King.

When the night time comes
And the star's bright glee
My eyes can no longer see
And physically beside you
I can no longer be
If you must cry for me
Find comfort in knowing
I am in glory
Listening to the Angels sing
Unto our King....

We Can Still Overcome Someday
SPEECH

When will someday come for us to overcome?
How can the Lord see us through someday,
When today does not find us doing the things
In which will see us overcoming someday?
How can victory be won someday;
When we don't even respect our forefathers
Who battled for us to overcome someday?

Not just battled; but were killed by the very hands;
In which they fought so hard to put in place
Avenues which could/would find themselves
Overcoming, poverty; overcoming ignorance;
Overcoming being thought as last! Pardon my French,
But it is a damn shame that the very ones trying
To help make someday reality, are the very ones
Being lied on, talked about, put down, persecuted;
And blatantly disrespected; not to mention;
Yet again; killed DEAD? That is pure foolishness!

So, let us pull up your pants men! Women let us put our
Damn clothes back on! Let us drop the drugs and guns
Out of our hands and replace all of that nonsense with
Some of the tools which will teach us all about someday!
Like the Bible! Let us educate ourselves while using our hands
To feed ourselves; instead for robbing, stealing; killing to get
To someday! Don't we understand people were brutally
Murdered just so we could be the ones living in some day?

When will understanding come to the mere fact,
The Lord is waiting to see us through to someday?
But how can He, when we refuse to see the
Bare naked truth which blocks our way leading

To someday? The same path which has already been
Laid to lead us all straight in to the blessings waiting
In someday, but; however, is being totally ignored as
Another passage way is being constructed to lead us
Through the valley of death! Yes; it is a wicked path;
One which is leading all of us into damnation/HELL, for
Disobedience causes the Lord to rain on the just
Well so as the unjust, my friends!

What "mine eyes" see today is not what the eyes
Of a greater leader saw many years ago as he
Stood before millions and spoke of someday!
In fact, I am afraid, because today, we are not
Walking hand and hand. The division seen is
Horrific! No love leading the way to someday!
Just the same old "Drum major instinct", preached
In a sermon by that very same leader! My God!
If the truth is what it will take to find us all;
Regardless of the pigmentation of our outer
Appearance; and regardless of the actions of our
Moral capability; standing in the ramifications
Of what someday truly; truly means, then lend
Me your ears; for deep in the pulse of my heart, I do believe
We can still overcome; someday!

<u>We Can Still Overcome Some Day</u>

Hymnal

We can still overcome some day!

We can still overcome some day!

We can still overcome some day!

If we believe; in the Father and the Son,
We can still overcome some day!

WE WELCOME YOU IN

Hallelujah Jesus! Hallelujah Jesus!
Hallelujah Jesus! Hallelujah Jesus!
Somebody needs You today Lord!
Somebody needs You today Lord!
Somebody needs You today Lord!
Somebody really need You today Lord!

Somebody woke up homeless!
Somebody woke up hungry!
Somebody woke up lonely!
Somebody didn't wake up at all!
Hallelujah Jesus! Hallelujah Jesus!

We really need You today.
To take all our pains away!
Yes to take away all of our sorrows!
Hallelujah Jesus! Hallelujah Jesus!
Hallelujah Jesus! Hallelujah Jesus!

We welcome You in!
We welcome You in!
We welcome You in!
Yes we welcome You in!

To save! To deliver!
To strengthen, to renew!

We welcome You in!
We welcome You in!
We welcome You in!
Yes we welcome You in Jesus!

WHAT HAVE YOU MADE IT THROUGH

What is your testimony?
What have you been through?
What is it that have made you cry,
When no one was looking at you?
As a child were you molested?
And then threatened not to tell?
But when you did, no one cared;
By responding, oh well?
What is your testimony?
Everyone has one, or two, or three?
Especially, if you're up in age.
Something has surely happened,
To bring you to your knees!
Was it pain from the sudden death of a love one?
Did it leave your heart numb? Such a tragedy!
Maybe it was enduring beatings;
From the hands of another,
Whose explanation for doing so,
Was proclaiming because I love you!
What is your testimony?
Have you ever been called dumb,
By your mother, sister, or brother,
Because of them being mad at you
For looking like your dead beat father?
Or maybe it just was being disappointed by family;
And friends, over and over again?
Perhaps, it was a bad marriage or a wayward child,
Which took away your smile, then brought you to your knees;
Crying out loud, Lord help me please? Such calamity!
What is your testimony?
Prayerfully it's that you turned things upside down,
From all of the negativity once holding you bound!
An inspirational message of you can do it too!
Just don't give up on God, because;
He never will give up on you!
What is your testimony?
What have you made it through?

WHAT IS IT LORD YOU NEED ME TO DO

Lord what is it You would have me to do
Which could substitute as proof
To how much I adore You
And how much it is I love You too?
Is there anything I can say
When down on my knees I pray
Something that would make all doubt flee?
That's right, You already understand my sincerity
How much in me I desire You are well pleased.
Lord, where is it You would have me to go
To let others know Your love for them is no joke
And that Jesus really died on cross for souls that were lost?
Lord grant me derivative vision so through Your eyes
I might be able to see the invisible plans
Which were written for me by Your hands.
Take me by my hands Lord and guide me to where I am to go
So once there, I will know for sure, You are there with me to!
I have got a made up mind to serve You Master God
And serve You is what I shall choose
So, what is it Lord, You need me to do?

Where I Am

I'm patiently waiting
In the midst of my troubles
Jesus for You to come
And take me by my hand
Because my faith it tells me
This is not in Your plans
For me to stay in this hurt
Where I am

Right where I am
Right where I am
I don't believe
You want me to stay
Where I am

So, I'm seeking and praying
Yes, I'm fasting and believing
Jesus one day You will come
To set me free
No I'm not worried
Because Your word tells me
You don't want me in this hurt
Where I am

Right where I am
Right where I am
Jesus I know
You don't want me
Where I am

Right where I am
Right where I am
I know You don't
Want me in this hurt
Where I am

WHO GETS ALL OF THE PRAISE

God, I would climb down the steepest mountain,
Just to boldly tell Your people to be still.
I would vehemently make sure they know
The message You instructed me to share is real.
Without stutter, I would not hesitate
Every word You gave to me, Lord I would say
Yes and proudly proclaim
So it is You God who gets all of the praise!
God I would build the biggest boat ever built,
And make sure to Your eyes it appeals.
Every board, every screw, every rail
Every rope, every window, every nail
Would be used Lord exactly how to me You tell
Then right before in it I set sail;
Every room would be checked to make sure it is filled
According to Your most perfect will,
So it is You God, who gets all of the praise!
Why would I vow to do such things?
When I know how much hardship it will bring?
It's because I understand, it's not about me
But all about the Son of Man
Who gave His life to follow Your plan
So it is You, God, who gets all of the praise!

~Women Do We Really Know Our Worth~

Women, do we really know our worth?
Someone viewed- not as last, but first!
Second after God, now, for He
Is the Maker and Creator of, all our hearts.
But to everyone else, quickly take a left.
Don't we understand, the reason we even
Exist, is solely to be - a strong tower,
Meaning we are strong enough to,
Meet the needs of one man, hour after hour;
Yes, the very same male figure whose rib
God formed us from, then, so impressed with the
Masterpiece made, while asleep man laid,
Patted Himself on the back and said;
This is a "good thing" - well done?

Women, do we really know our worth?
How man can't live without us on this earth?
Does it mean we should be catering
To secret fantasies? Talk to the rib!
Of course - not! Because God only
Pulled one rib from its slot; not two or three.
Besides, take it from Eve! Did she need any help,
Convincing Adam to eat the fig, from her tree?
Please! Don't keep being so weak!
Fearfully, wonderfully, beautifully, seductively,
Patiently made! So when looked upon by the
Eyes of your man, he does everything he can;
To reassure - it is God, Who gets all of the praise;
For his precious gift; his "good thing", his Woman!
Women, do we really know our worth?

Your Power Lord

Lord place Your power
Deep inside of me
Your spiritual power
A light for the whole world to see
May the energy flow so
Oh and touch every need
Then replace it with Your love
Yes and Your mercy
Lord place Your power in me

So I can serve You
Lord so I can serve You
The way that You need me to do
So I can be a light shining bright
Lord place Your power in me

I feel it working, working, working; working
Your power Lord
I feel it healing, healing, healing; healing
Your power Lord
I feel it saving, saving, saving, saving
Your power Lord
Your power Lord, You placed in me

Believers, in God, through Christ Jesus

…..did you know sin is beautiful? Did you know sin is captivating? Did you know sin brings the flesh much pleasure? Yes, of course it is and does. In order for the adversary to lure one in to sin, he made or makes it pleasing to the eyes. Even though to sin is an ugly thing, no one would be a willing participant of it if it really was an ugly thing. Do you think Eve would have been able to convince Adam to sin against what God told him not to do if she was not a beautiful sight to behold? Of course not.

Sin is easy to get into and hard to get out of. This is why God says in His words (Ecclesiastics 21:2) to "flee from sin as from the face of a serpent". This means run away from it. Don't reason with it. When you see it coming, go the other way. Get the heck out of dodge! LOL! It's funny, but then, again, it's not as a believer of Christ Jesus, because God also requires us in His words, to deny ourselves daily (Mark 8:34-35) if it is truly Him in which we are following. In other words, no matter how difficult it is not to sin, there would be no desire to entertain the perils of sin, for we know, as a true professed believer, sin must be gone in order to not just follow, but, to find the True and Living God to follow. Besides, God also tells us in His word, "the wages of sin, is death but the gift of God is eternal life through Jesus Christ our Lord" (Romans 6:23). ~Amen~

…..how are we representing God and Jesus? Are we standing up for them like they left instructions for us to do as believers in them? Why are we praying? Why are we going to church? Why are we professing to be a believer? We might as well go join the sinners if we are not going to stand up for that which Jesus laid down for! ~Amen~

…..we are living in a world today where the people who are striving to do right are the ones looked down and frowned upon, while the blatant sinners are the ones who are celebrated! Here's the thing though, both categories are claiming to be believing in the Christ Jesus in which the Holy Bible speaks of.

If we, as believers, are not already studying the Holy Bible and desire to know the truth, then it is strongly suggested to start studying to showing ourselves approved unto God, ASAP, for, it is in learning we will find out, professed believer, God has already begin to show, He is not pleased with the way this world is falling prey to the sin in which He so despises! ~Amen~

…..did you know after all Moses did to save God's people from out of bondage, when the time came for the slave master, Pharaoh, to let God's people go and follow Moses, straight out of the wilderness, some of them did not go? Did you know after all of Moses sacrificing, once out of burden, most of the freed rebelled? Did you know for their ungratefulness, God put all of them back in the wilderness for 40 years? Did you know this included Moses too? (Book of Exodus) (Numbers 32:13) ~Amen~

…..did you know there will be no haters allowed in heaven, especially since the biggest hater of all and his followers, were kicked out, by God, a long, long, time ago? (Romans 2 & Isaiah 12-32) ~Amen~

…our belief, no matter how much we yell, scream, run, jump, shout, or holler we love God, through Jesus, becomes null and void, if we are not living a life according to God, through Christ Jesus. ~Amen~

…..if we start praying and thanking God for the air we breathe, and for being able to wake up framed in our right minds, and for being able to claim a reasonable portion of good health, and for having hands that desire to work, even though right now there is no work, then maybe, just maybe, it might be the reason for Him deciding to go ahead and add all the other things prayed for unto our lives. (Matthew 6:33) ~Amen~

…..salvation is about our service, not our shout! ~Amen~

…..some of us are looking to the wrong hills for our help!" ~Amen~

Thanks for your support!
"After Another Chance" has been granted by God, to become a faithful servant in His Kingdom, the next step taken by the humble heart, is to be prepared to climb even higher in your purpose! So with that being said, got to go!

See you at the top family & friends...

Dorothy A. Cooper

Look for Dorothy's first book:

Another Chance

Amazon.com

You can contact and find more information on

Dorothy A. Cooper

On Facebook:

https://www.facebook.com/DADysonCooper

And At:

Scan to view my Website!

katrinasworks.com

www.ingramcontent.com/pod-product-compliance
Lightning Source LLC
Chambersburg PA
CBHW041525090426
42736CB00035B/16